180°

TURNAROUND

180°

TURNAROUND

FROM MERELY EXISTING TO TRULY LIVING

BY LAWRENCE NEISENT

TATE PUBLISHING
AND ENTERPRISES, LLC

Published by Tate Publishing & Enterprises, LLC
127 E. Trade Center Terrace | Mustang, Oklahoma 73064 USA
1.888.361.9473 | www.tatepublishing.com

Tate Publishing is committed to excellence in the publishing industry. The company reflects the philosophy established by the founders, based on Psalm 68:11,
"The Lord gave the word and great was the company of those who published it."

Book design copyright © 2013 by Tate Publishing, LLC. All rights reserved.
Cover design by Samson Lim
Interior design by Caypeeline Casas

Published in the United States of America

ISBN: 978-1-62510-832-6
1. Religion / Christian Life / General
2. Self-Help / Spiritual
13.03.18

TABLE OF CONTENTS

FOREWORD

In May 2012, my son-in-law Glen and I had the privilege of staying with the Neisent family for a few days. Though I was there to minister in the church, some of my fondest memories had to do with becoming part of the family. Glen and I got pummeled with pillows by Faith and Lexi and regularly took part in water fights. We enjoyed sitting down watching a movie and consuming popcorn. We also walked into an atmosphere of shalom where daily devotions, good food, and stimulating conversation were part of the culture.

We were therefore not surprised when we became part of the church community that a similar way of doing things created an atmosphere where the presence of God was welcomed.

Over the years, I've read many Christian books, but this one for me is a reflection of what has been accomplished in the life of the church there and particularly in the Neisent family. Paul, when writing to the Corinthian Church writes, "You yourselves are our letter, written on our hearts and read by everyone" (2 Cor 3:2, NIV, 1984).

This book speaks into your potential and the potential of the church community. Lawrence writes, "It's not what you are that holds you back, it's what you think you're not." One of the hardest things to establish in a church is a kingdom culture. Please read a chapter at a time, giving space in between for meditation and thought, and if taken seriously, it will change the way you are forever. This is a book not only well written but well modeled.

Stuart Bell

INTRODUCTION

Can you really change?

After a lion is caged long enough, he doesn't even believe he's a lion anymore.

Whatever has confined you in your life can only hold you captive if you continue to allow it to confine you. It's time to break into new dimensions of life and freedom.

> Therefore if anyone is in Christ, he is a new creature; the old things passed away; behold, new things have come.
>
> 2 Cor 5:17 (NASB)

New things have come! With God, our transformation is a lifelong process that is filled with joy, hope, and anticipation of more that he has in store. The mercies of the Lord are new every morning because he's constantly taking us to new places. Expect it! Believe it!

Change is all about a culture shift. You can experience the inspiration to change without ever addressing the culture of your life. After some time, inspiration fades, and the culture prevails like ruts on a well-traveled road that keep you held on course. Don't lose hope!

Shifting your culture is like steering a ship. At first, it appears that not much is going on. But then, steadily, over time, there begins to be a noticeable change in the scenery. Before you know what happened, the course of your life has been altered, and you will never be the same.

This book is filled with stories of people who have really changed. Change begins with a thought that seeds the idea. The idea sustained produces an attitude. The attitude sustained produces an atmosphere of your life. The atmosphere sustained produces a climate, and the climate sustained produces a culture. It's this renewed culture that prevails like ruts in a well-traveled road, holding you on course when temptation tries to take you away.

Galatians 6 speaks of the law of sowing and reaping. This law isn't a law God designed to bring a curse. The law of sowing and reaping was designed by God to multiply the blessings in your life.

God is in the business of 180-Degree Turnarounds. After all, it was a murderer named Saul who turned around after meeting Christ and was given the new name, Paul. He then wrote the book of Galatians, which talks about the law of sowing and reaping.

According to Paul, people change when they meet Jesus. He's also the divinely inspired writer of Corinthians.

> Therefore if anyone is in Christ, he is a new creature; the old things passed away; behold, new things have come.

> 2 Cor 5:17 (NASB)

~

Nathan was only seventeen but already on a path to disaster and despair. At one point in his young life, he was taking meth on a daily basis. He had stolen guns from his father to support his habit. His violent tendencies included knocking holes in the doors of his parents' home, destroying furniture, and even attacking his father in fits of rage. One day, when his mom was giving him a ride, she mentioned that she was praying for Nathan. He became violent and began throwing some of her things out of the car window. In his rage, he even broke the windshield with his fist. The situation looked hopeless.

Today, Nathan is a loving husband and father to four. He is a pastor on our staff at the church where I am the lead pastor, Destiny Christian Center, and is not the same person he used to be. Nathan is one of the people you will meet in this book, as we look at how Jesus reaches into our lives and transforms us one thought at a time. His loving process changes the culture in our hearts, making an incredible difference in our future.

Thoughtfully and prayerfully consider this progression, as you read each story and think of your own life journey. Nathan's 180-Degree Turnaround—moving from merely existing to truly living—came as a result of progressively transforming the culture of his life.

Making Your 180-Degree Turnaround:

What one area in my life do I need to invite God's transforming power into so I can become more like Jesus?

What one thing tends to hold me back in this area of my life?

What one verse could I memorize and rehearse to gain strength in this area of my life?

180° TURNAROUND

THE PROCESS OF CHANGE

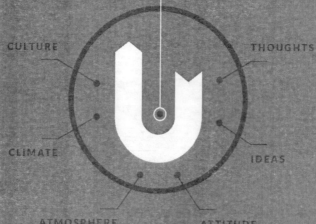

CULTURE

THOUGHTS

CLIMATE

IDEAS

ATMOSPHERE

ATTITUDE

Thoughts sustained produce ideas. Ideas sustained produce attitudes. Attitudes sustained produce an atmosphere. Atmosphere sustained produces a climate. Climate sustained produces culture. Culture resulting from the thoughts and wisdom of God is the expression of God's Kingdom in the earth through our surrendered lives!

THE PROCESS OF CHANGE

Mark Twain said, "It's easy to quit smoking. I've done it hundreds of times."

Change is one of the most misunderstood concepts in our world. If you're still struggling in an area of your life, it's a sure sign that you are not yet defeated. Don't give up! Don't give in! Keep fighting and keep struggling! You're making more progress than you might think.

Our transformed lives become the expression to our world that God's Kingdom has come! The ability to change is the one ability that separates mankind from all other creation. Cows eat grass and will never change their own diet. Birds fly south and will never make alternate vacation plans. Trees bud when spring-like conditions tell them to do so. *People don't change unless they understand how to address the culture of their lives.*

Change your culture, change your future.

A few years ago, my family had the opportunity to travel to China with friends. During our stay, one day, we took a taxi from the hotel to get out and experience the culture of Beijing. My daughters Faith and Lexi, then aged nine and ten, were very excited to see the Chinese acrobats performing downtown. At one point in our adventure, we found ourselves walking down an alley that was packed with people and filled with vendors displaying more food than a state fair! Some items we recognized and some we did not. A variety of insects on sticks were among the available delicacies.

As we approached one booth, I observed skewers of scorpions in groups of three. I was shocked to see a slight movement. I blew on this arranged bouquet of critters, and all of them responded with creepy crawling motion. My wife and girls all screamed at this surprising revelation. My American friend Ryan and I decided to taste this delicious treat. Okay, it's not what I would call delicious, but we did try scorpion that evening right there in some back alley in Beijing, China!

Every nation has a culture of its own. There are regional cultures within nations. The southern United States region is known for hospitality and for certain foods like okra, black-eyed peas, and fried green tomatoes. There are cultural distinctions within cities—various parts of any city can become known as the arts district, the business district, or any other cultural distinctive. Every home in every neighborhood has its own culture.

Culture is the progression of thoughts and ideas that lead to attitudes, which produce an influencing atmosphere by which a person, family, city or region becomes known. Thoughts are the seeds of culture.

Thoughts of friendliness produce a culture of friendliness. People who have an atmosphere of friendliness draw other people in like Tigger from the *Winnie the Pooh* series. There are also those who carry an atmosphere of heaviness, like Eeyore. Remember his greeting to Pooh Bear, "Good morning, Pooh Bear, if it is a good morning, which I doubt."

The culture of a person's life can be understood and addressed, if we peel back the layers of attitudes and ideas, which reveal the seeds of thoughts that produced them. Once we understand this process, we can effectively initiate the *process of change*.

Change is a process, not an event.

Good habits are as easy to form as bad ones. We develop bad habits through continued repetition. In the same way, we are fully capable of filling our lives with good habits.

Our brains are part computer and part chemical factory, responding to stimulations and impulses that create neurological connections. The brain is a collection of billions of interconnected neurons. Each neuron is a cell that uses biochemical reactions to receive, process, and transmit information, integrating experiences with memories. There are even chemical rewards assigned to pleasurable or favorable experiences, making strong neurological connections on a cellular level. There are also negative chemical releases that occur as a result of neurological connections dealing with fear, stress, or other negative emotions.

Habits, patterns, and addictions all have the same developmental process. This God-ordained, habit-forming mechanism in every person is part of His plan to empower us for our future. The Bible teaches us to be transformed by the renewing of our minds (Rom 12:2). The developmental process of habit-forming is so powerfully fortified with God's design of chemical release and rewards to our system that God reveals it as a law. The law of sowing and reaping is actually intended to empower you for your God-given destiny, as a result of Christ-centered thinking.

The first time a gymnast stands on a balance beam, the struggle is obvious—arms turning, twisting and waving to keep her balance. However, with enough practice, that same person can do unimaginable maneuvers with ease and confidence. Everybody falls down the first time they try to walk. In life, we learn that everything is hard until it's easy. This works both ways—good and bad. The first time a person tells a lie, their heart races, and nervousness abounds. Whatever you keep doing eventually gets easier.

Practice makes perfect, so be careful what you practice.

The interaction with and the application of God's living word will take us into another dimension of life. It's not merely the truth that sets us free. It's *knowing the truth* that sets us free.

> Then you will know the truth, and the truth will set you free.
>
> John 8:32 (NIV)

The process of change begins with knowing and practicing fresh thoughts of hope. *Thoughts* sustained produce ideas. *Ideas* sustained produce attitudes that become deeply rooted in our hearts. *Attitudes* sustained produce an atmosphere about our lives by which we become known. *Atmosphere* sustained produces a climate that affects the lives of people around us. *Climate* sustained produces culture that becomes our legacy that lives on long after we are gone.

Thoughts are to culture what seeds are to forests.

∼

At age twenty-seven, Barbara was drinking heavily, using cocaine, and other drugs. She frequently sold drugs to support her habits. Her pursuit of men never fulfilled her need for love. Men and drugs only masked the emptiness of her soul.

Barbara came to know Christ, and today is a wife and mother of two daughters, which she raised in the church. She is a vital part of our Destiny staff. God not only changed who Barbara was, but he surrounded her with an atmosphere of peace and joy. When you call our office, you'll hear her compassionate and loving voice. God's love changes our ways of thinking, one thought at a time.

Barbara's 180-Degree Turnaround came from a transformed culture. In order to move from merely existing to truly living, she had to address the *thoughts* that were responsible for the previous culture of her life.

Making Your 180-Degree Turnaround:

What area of my life have I been discouraged with because I didn't understand the process of change?

What are three things I can do to help cultivate a stronger process of change in this area?

Who is a trusted friend that I can share my struggle with so we can be praying for each other specifically?

THOUGHTS

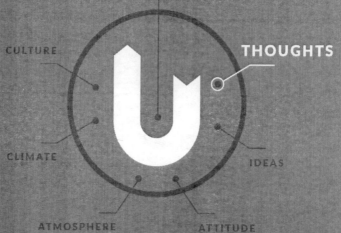

THE PROCESS OF CHANGE

CULTURE

THOUGHTS

CLIMATE

IDEAS

ATMOSPHERE

ATTITUDE

THOUGHTS

If you watch what you think,
you won't have to watch what you say.

"Law office, this is Darla. May I help you?" is the response that comes every time my mom answers the ringing phone at her office. One day, I called her home phone and was greeted with this same standard work greeting. As the last word rolled off of her tongue, she realized what she'd done, and laughter abounded on both ends of the conversation. The rehearsed greeting had become so embedded in her thought process that it came out without her even thinking about it. The ability to train the brain is a very fascinating part of our God-given design. This emerges in our lives in a variety of ways.

Over the course of three years, I left my office to go home an estimated one thousand times, driving twenty minutes south to pull into my drive. Then, we moved to a different house, and the journey became twenty minutes north. My brain had been trained by one thousand repetitions to go what was now redefined as "the wrong direction." Finally, it happened. I found myself almost "home" before I realized I'd been driving away from home the entire time.

Habits are a series of steps learned gradually and sometimes without conscious awareness. Repeated habits ultimately become the culture of your life. This is precisely why we are cautioned by God in His Word to guard our hearts. The culture of your life is being established either purposefully or accidentally. *Just as your thoughts produce your culture, your decisions determine your destiny.* When something gets in your heart, it's only a matter of time before it shows up in your future.

> Above all else, guard your heart, for it is the well-spring of life.
>
> Proverbs 4:23 (NIV, 1984)

The wellspring of life that exists in the heart is part of man's uniquely contagious design. Once you start on a familiar series of actions, you stop thinking about them, and you're able to complete them without conscious thought or attention. We are designed for habits of holiness and patterns of purity. The fall of mankind caused us to malfunction, and this produced dysfunction in what should come naturally. Renewing our minds continually to God's Word brings restoration to God's original intentions for our lives. We literally begin participating in the divine nature of God, and the culture of God's Kingdom is restored to our lives.

> His divine power has given us everything we need for life and godliness through our knowledge of

him who called us by his own glory and goodness. Through these he has given us his very great and precious promises, so that through them you may participate in the divine nature and escape the corruption in the world caused by evil desires.

2 Peter 1:3–4 (NIV)

Your mind will frustrate your anointing if you don't renew it with God's Word! God's Word introduces you to thoughts of God's logic. John 1 reveals that Jesus came into our fallen world as a revelation of God's logic that we can personally and intimately embrace.

In the beginning was the Word, and the Word was with God, and the Word was God.

John 1:1 (NIV)

The Greek word that translates "word" in this text is *logos*. In English, *logos* is the root of "logic." In the Greek language, *logos* extends beyond the idea of a mere word. This actually reveals God's desire to introduce the world to God's way of thinking—His logic—giving a much more elaborate idea than a single word. *Logos* speaks of language, talking, conversation, story, thought, and reason.

God addressed the world's dysfunction by sending "the Word," or God's logic embodied in Christ. God continues to address man's dysfunction in this same way. Your mind must be made ready to operate on the level of your anointing or deficiencies will produce dysfunction and will rob you of God's best.

> As for you, you were dead in your transgressions and sins, in which you used to live when you followed the ways of this world and of the ruler of the kingdom of the air, the spirit who is now at work in those who are disobedient. All of us also lived among them at one time, gratifying the cravings of our sinful nature and following its desires and thoughts. Like the rest, we were by nature objects of wrath.

> Ephesians 2:1–3 (NIV)

In the Old Testament, the enemy was trying to contaminate the bloodline of the Messiah to derail God's plan of redemption. God's command to kill all enemies when conquering a land is difficult to understand, unless we recognize that it was all to protect the lineage of Christ. When Jesus came, there was a stark transition that took place, and our battle became clearly defined in Ephesians 6 as a battle that was not against flesh and blood. In 2 Corinthians 10, Paul describes a fight with weapons that demolish ideologies that are contrary to the knowledge of God. The enemy is still trying to derail God's plan of redemption. Now that Jesus has come, and God's Kingdom logic has been released, the plan is to use tactics of ignorance on individuals. This is why God's people are destroyed for lack of knowledge (Hosea 4:6).

> The weapons we fight with are not the weapons of the world. On the contrary, they have divine power to demolish strongholds. We demolish arguments and every pretension that sets itself up against the knowledge of God, and we take captive every thought to make it obedient to Christ.
>
> 2 Corinthians 10:4–5 (NIV)

The New Testament battle is just as fierce as the Old Testament battles. However, the New Testament battle is now fought in efforts to preserve the lineage of Christ in our own lives by taking thoughts captive. *Our minds must be made ready to operate on the level of our anointing, or we are surrendering to the fall of mankind more than the resurrection of Christ.*

Our biggest battles are internal, not external. If we can win on the inside, we will win on the outside! If we don't fix the mind, everything invested leaks out as we automatically default to fallen tendencies and patterns. Being saved is one thing. But the next level is to allow the mind of Christ to dwell in our lives, establishing our jurisdiction, and shaping our destiny.

David fought like a warrior because David thought like a warrior.

God's purposes are always greater than our problems. We must keep working at living life without magnifying problems more than we magnify God. To magnify is to make bigger. Problems get bigger in your mind as you rehearse them. Stop rehearsing your mountain to your God, and start rehearsing your God to your mountain! Magnify God, focus on his greatness, and he gets bigger in your mind than any situation you face.

> O magnify the LORD with me, And let us exalt His name together.
>
> Psalm 34:3 (NASB)

Pause here to magnify the Lord for his ability to remove the mountains in your life. Magnifying the mountain is the basis for discouragement. Magnifying God is the basis for breaking into new places of faith and courage.

Now, stop for a moment to consider three things in your life for which you are thankful to God.

Practicing thoughts of thankfulness when we're discouraged is vital to our future. The ability to replace discouraged thoughts with thankful thoughts is a sign of cultural health. Just as our bodies have vital signs, so does the culture of our lives. To check our cultural vital signs, we evaluate if we are able to give thanks when we're discouraged. We are what our brain eats, so we must beware of negative feasts.

The buzzard and the hummingbird both fly over the same desert. The buzzard searches for that which is rotting and died yesterday. The hummingbird searches for colorful and living blossoms. Both find what they're looking for. We all find what we look for in life. Discouragement holds your focus captive to death and disappointment. This is why we must dwell on thoughts of God's living word to find hope for a better future.

> For I know the thoughts that I think toward you, says the Lord, thoughts of peace and not of evil, to give you a future and a hope.
>
> Jeremiah 29:11 (NKJV)

God's thoughts inspire ideas of hope. Thoughts are seeded in our heads and *ideas* take root in our hearts.

~

Sharon was saved at a young age, loved God, and volunteered in church. She was a "model Christian." But deep beneath the obvious, she was experiencing pain, shame, anger, and depression stemming from childhood sexual abuse and years of seeing her father physically abuse her mother. There were times when she felt she couldn't go on, but she had been taught that good Christians suffer in silence.

In one of Sharon's efforts to "do the right thing," she joined a women's Bible study group for people with hurts, habits, and hang-ups. When Sharon admitted her painful past and asked for prayer her whole life changed, and her heart was healed. She was *set free*. She couldn't stop smiling. Today, Sharon understands how much God loves her, volunteers with joy, and lives in faith that "whom the son sets free is free indeed!"

Sharon's 180-Degree Turnaround comes from a transformed culture. To move from merely existing to truly living, she had to address the *ideas* that were strengthening the previous culture of her life.

Making Your 180-Degree Turnaround:

What area of your life is being sabotaged by wrong ways of thinking?

What do you believe is God's way of thinking about this area of your life?

What practical thing can you do to more effectively remember to practice God's thoughts in this area of your life? (Phone reminders, Scripture written on index card you carry in your pocket, etc)

LAWRENCE NEISENT

IDEAS

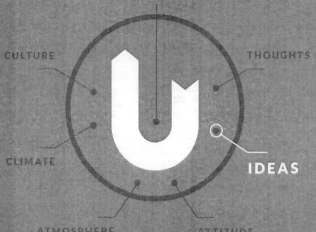

THE PROCESS OF CHANGE

CULTURE

THOUGHTS

CLIMATE

IDEAS

ATMOSPHERE

ATTITUDE

IDEAS

Weeds had started growing in our backyard, but it was easier to neglect them than to address the problem. One day, I noticed that one of my unwanted yard guests was becoming stronger and seemingly more prevalent. I had neglected them long enough and it was past time to confront my weed issues. I announced to my family that I was going out to pull the weeds, but I had no idea what was before me. At six feet and one inch tall, I courageously led my eleven-year-old daughter to the battlefield, towering over my fifteen-inch tall opponent. I was prepared to triumph quickly and victoriously. I grabbed this flimsy plant not knowing I was about to have my first wrestling match with a baby oak tree. This sapling oak had roots beneath the obvious that were longer than its height above the ground. Eventually, I was victorious, though I had quite the struggle, breaking a sweat, and making grunting sounds that caused my daughter to laugh at her conquering warrior of a father!

It seems that a lot of us have weeds growing secretly in our backyards that are easier to neglect than to address. Neglecting them allows roots to grow beneath the obvious in our lives. The obvious is how we behave. The not so obvious is what we believe. What we believe determines how we behave. Clearly, the obvious results from a secretly hidden root structure of ideas that exist in our hearts.

What seeds in the mind takes root in the heart.

Ideas are thoughts, good or bad, that have been allowed to grow in the brain and extend roots into the heart. Plucking thoughts from the soil of our lives is an easier task if done early in the life of the thought. If a thought remains in the soil of our lives for very long it can only be addressed effectively at the roots. Good thoughts produce healthy roots and bad thoughts produce unhealthy roots. Ideas are like deep-rooted oak trees that slowly grow in a person's life.

When a child comes home from school expressing ideas that are contrary to the culture of a home, a quick reaction is, "Who put that idea in your head?" Ideas have the power to change culture if they are allowed to survive. Ideas left unchecked begin growing in your home as trees grow in your yard.

Practice makes perfect, so you better be careful what you practice.

As Isaiah spoke of Israel's deliverance, he said, "In days to come Jacob will take root, Israel will bud and blossom and fill all the world with fruit" (Isa 27:6, NIV). It's interesting that Jacob, which means deceiver, takes root beneath the obvious and Israel, which means "God strives" or "saved by God" bears fruit above. If we are to live fruitful lives, we must address the deceiver in all of us in the secret and quiet places of God's presence.

As we endure tenaciously in places of prayer and God's Word, we develop a healthy root structure beneath the obvious. When our ideas become shaped by God's ideas, we begin to be rooted in righteousness as the culture of our lives. "I have hidden your word in my heart that I might not sin against you." (Ps 119:11, NIV)

Good habits are as easy to form as bad ones.

Proverbs 23:7 (KJV) references man's thinking heart. Thinking heads lead to deeper ideas with an emotional attachment in a thinking heart. When emotions begin to be attached to beliefs, our defense system begins to preserve and protect them. This is the basis for losing the ability to be objective. We are all capable of being irrational.

A person can do something they know is completely wrong because their heart is more powerful than their head. Our hearts can be powerful and dangerous. "Follow your heart" is a common expression. The problem is that it's more of a cultural idea than a biblical idea. The Bible never says to follow your heart, but rather to guard your heart (Prov 4:23), because it can be such a powerful force in your life.

The human heart beats about eighty times every minute. This means the heart beats more than a hundred thousand times in a day, which translates to more than thirty-five million times in a year. The heart has an incredible physical mission, and its emotional mission is equally impressive.

When I watched my daughter receive the good citizen award, as a result of her fifth grade classmates voting, I felt as if my heart were tripling in size at that very moment! When somebody cut me off in traffic on my way home that same day, I felt my heart immediately changing again— only this time it was in the other direction. The heart is a powerful force in our lives. The Bible clearly teaches that the heart can be dangerous and desperately needs to be rooted in ideas expressed in God's Word.

> The heart is more deceitful than all else and is desperately sick; who can understand it?
>
> Jeremiah 17:9 (NASB)

Deeply rooted ideas not only have the power to transform our lives, but they also have the power to transform our world. The idea of democracy in our world today was not the result of great thinkers of the 1700s. The idea of democracy is actually traced back to ancient Athens, around 508 BC.[1] Philosophers from all over the Greek world gathered to develop their theories. Aristotle said, "…(in) the principle of justice prevailing, the multitude must of necessity be sovereign and the decision of the majority must be final and must constitute justice…"[2] Ideas can change your world.

Great ideas have the power to move us. Bad ideas have the power to ruin us. God's ideas have the power to transform us! Within you, right now, is the power to do things you never dreamed possible. Your potential can be achieved as soon as you change your ideas. It's not what you are that holds you back. It's what you think you're not. When you get your ideas right, the roots that are established in your heart hold you on course, no matter what storms and situations may come your way. Jesus said he was the fulfillment of Isaiah 61 as he came to reverse the curse and establish people as deeply rooted "oaks of righteousness."

> The Spirit of the Sovereign LORD is on me, because the LORD has anointed me to preach good news to the poor. He has sent me to bind up the brokenhearted, to proclaim freedom for the captives and release from darkness for the prisoners, to proclaim the year of the LORD's favor and the day of vengeance of our God, to comfort all who mourn, and provide for those who grieve in Zion—to bestow on them a crown of beauty instead of ashes, the oil of gladness instead of mourning, and a garment of praise instead of a spirit of despair. They will be called oaks of righteousness, a planting of the LORD for the display of his splendor.
>
> Isaiah 61:1–3 (NIV)

The seeds of ideas produce a root structure in our lives that the Bible calls strongholds. Strongholds can be good if aligned with God's Word, or strongholds can be bad if they are contrary to God's Word. Ideas that continue to deepen their roots and grow in our lives will be revealed in the *attitudes* of our hearts.

~

At the age of thirteen, Trudi began a lifestyle of alcohol, marijuana, speed, cocaine, and acid. Trudi had her first abortion at the age of fourteen, and her second at eighteen. After marrying and having two children, but still no relief from depression, she began attending AA (Alcoholics Anonymous) meetings. Years later, after entering a rehab facility, she was taking more than thirty prescription pills each day. After twenty-six years of marriage, her husband admitted he was having an affair with her best friend, and they divorced.

Walking through all of this, she came to know Christ, who has kept her through the process of conquering depression, unforgiveness, and total emptiness. Today, Trudi is one of the most contagiously fun and enjoyable people that you'll ever meet. Her influence to her friends, coworkers, and all of us at church is one that clothes others with attitudes of joy and encouragement.

The 180-Degree Turnaround in the culture of Trudi's life occurred as she confronted the *attitude* that kept her merely existing rather than truly living.

Making Your 180-Degree Turnaround:

What ideas do you hold that tend to hold you on a course that needs to change?

Who do you know that tends to have the right ideas in this area of life?

How can you reach out to this person with the right ideas asking them to speak effectively into your life as a mentor?

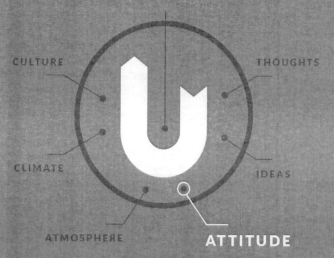

ATTITUDE

THE PROCESS OF CHANGE

CULTURE

THOUGHTS

CLIMATE

IDEAS

ATMOSPHERE

ATTITUDE

ATTITUDE

Everybody has attitude. There are good attitudes and bad attitudes. There are happy attitudes and sad attitudes. There are considerate attitudes and grumpy attitudes. Positive thoughts develop positive ideas and grow positive attitudes. Preserving a positive attitude in a fallen world takes a constant commitment to practice a perspective of hope.

After enough begging from my girls, I finally gave in. We set up a fish tank in their bedroom, and they were so excited with their new pets. Days passed, and the excitement wore off. Weeks passed, and there had to be reminders to feed the fish. Months passed, and I was fed up with the fish smell emanating from the bedroom every time I walked down the hallway.

Cautiously, I began to formulate a plan that would be quite an accomplishment on my "dad" resume. I began dropping hints. My four– and five-year-old daughters were sly to my tactics by this age. Finally, after enough discussions about how much work the fish had become; after what seemed like the five hundredth time tank cleaning; after several reminders to the girls about how much more simple life was BF (before fish); it was time.

I gathered the family together for a special movie night. I prepared the popcorn, and then unveiled the featured presentation, *Finding Nemo*! It couldn't have been a more perfect setting. I concluded the movie with a discussion about these poor tropical fish we were holding captive and how they needed to go find their family in the lake near our house.

At last, the girls agreed that the fish should be set free. We made our way the very next day to the boat dock. The girls were very excited! We got out of the car, and I carefully carried these orphaned fish that were about to find their long lost families. "Nemo is coming home!" I shouted as the girls and I walked toward the water. They were very pleased at this wonderful deed that their noble father was performing right before their eyes!

Carefully, I put the precious little foster fish back into the water, setting them free. Suddenly, it happened. Five ducks appeared from behind the dock, thinking we were there to feed them. They quickly swam right up to us and ate Blackie. Then, they shamelessly and without conscience, continued by eating Goldie.

With very few options, I shouted very loudly, "Wow! How awesome is that? We got to let the fish go and feed the ducks all at the same time! Let's go tell mom!" My young daughters responded in stunned silence, searching for the appropriate attitude. Finally, they yelled, "Yeah! Hurry! Let's go tell mom!"

We've all heard that when life gives you lemons you should make lemonade. The truth is, however, the lemons life gives us tend to already be in our mouths before we have a chance to respond. The natural thing to do is to pucker and make a horrible face. Translating unexpected and difficult situations into hopeful circumstances takes constant practice of an established attitude.

Life is not about what happens to you. Life is about what happens in you when things happen to you.

Babe Ruth is known as the home run king. Interestingly enough, he had almost twice as many strikeouts as he had home runs. Why isn't he called the strikeout king? The reason is because the home runs were counted and the strikeouts were not. Life is about learning to count correctly. Don't let your strikeouts get you down. Get back up to that plate and swing for another home run! Marriages fail because they focus on strikeouts. People grow discouraged in their careers because they focus on the strikeouts.

Successful people are not those who have never experienced failure. Successful people learn from their mistakes. Thomas Edison is known as possibly the greatest inventor of all time. Eight out of ten of his inventions never worked. His attitude was one of constantly moving beyond mistakes to keep striving for a better future.

Circumstances are often out of your control, but your attitude is a hundred percent your responsibility. Don't let other people or situations choose your attitude for you.

Your attitude determines your altitude in almost every situation, so work on your attitude and increase your altitude.

The Beatles were turned down by Decca Recording Company for this reason: "We don't like your sound & guitar music is on the way out." Michael Jordan was cut from his high school basketball team "because he lacks skill." Walt Disney was fired from a newspaper because he "lacked imagination and has no original ideas."[1] Statistically, we fail more than we succeed. So, how we handle failure is directly linked to our ability to succeed. Failure becomes fertilizer when we allow it to help us grow.

Once a reporter asked Edison how it made him feel to have had one thousand failed experiments when trying to invent the light bulb. Edison responded, "They weren't failed experiments. Successfully inventing the light bulb was a 1,000 step process." At age sixty-seven, Edison lost all of his work to a fire that completely burned his factory to the ground. The next morning, as he walked through the ashes, he is quoted as saying, "There is great value in disaster. All of our mistakes are burned up. Thank God we can start anew." Three weeks later, the world's first phonograph was invented, and thousands more inventions would come before his death.[2]

Learning to manage the pain of disappointment and discouragement without growing despondent is vital to life, relationships, and leadership. One young pastor had introduced a variety of changes to a church just after arriving as their new pastor. Suddenly, the church began to grow, but not without opposition. One day, the young man stepped to his pulpit to find a card with the word "fool" waiting for him on his podium. As he picked it up before the entire congregation, he made an announcement. "Many times I've known a man to write a letter and not sign his name. This is the first time I've known a man to sign his name and not write the letter."

Our ability to cultivate thoughts and ideas into positive attitudes must never be underestimated. A study attributed to Harvard University revealed that 85 percent of the reasons for success, accomplishments, promotions, etc. were because of our attitudes, and only 15 percent because of education, intelligence, or talent. Incredibly talented people are overlooked every day because of their inability to get along with others. Attitude truly is everything!

The average child laughs about four hundred times every day while the average adult laughs about fifteen times a day.[3] Somewhere, over the course of life, we start letting our thoughts and ideas get pressurized, producing an attitude that doesn't smile as often as it should. Nobody stops laughing because they've grown old. They grow old because somewhere along their journey, they stopped laughing.

Attitude tends to be all about perspective. At the core, thoughts produce perspective, and perspective is very important. When you have the right perspective, peace abounds in your life. When you lose perspective, you're a mess. The devil doesn't have to tie you up for you to be bound. He just has to fill your head with thoughts and ideas of stress, worry, anger, unforgiveness, or low self-esteem. We are physically capable of sickness as a result of a contaminated attitude that lingers long enough.

Your attitude produces an *atmosphere* that affects not only your life, but the lives of everybody around you.

~

Rick was desperate, and driving aimlessly through the city asking, "Where can I go?" "Who can I talk to?" "Who can I trust?" Rick's wife told him she wanted a divorce, and he knew that this time she was finished. His addiction to pornography had controlled his life and finally was serving notice on his marriage. Their marriage had become another one of the many statistics of this problem that plagues our culture more than anybody wants to admit.

The process of restoration was slow, painful, and agonizing at times. Through honesty, transparency, and submission, Rick and Teri were not only able to stay together, but today, are an example of what Christ can do in a seemingly hopeless situation. This couple has become a very foundational family, providing leadership, guidance, and direction for many others in our Destiny church family. Rick effectively leads groups of men out of the bondage of addiction and into a right relationship with the Father. To God be the glory!

Rick's 180-Degree Turnaround came from a cultural transformation in his life and marriage. This only happened as a result of feeding a different *atmosphere* surrounding his life.

Making Your 180-Degree Turnaround:

What attitude do you hold that could be considered the greatest enemy to your future?

What attitude would be the best replacement for this bad attitude?

How can you connect more personally with someone you know that tends to carry this attitude you want in your life?

ATMOSPHERE

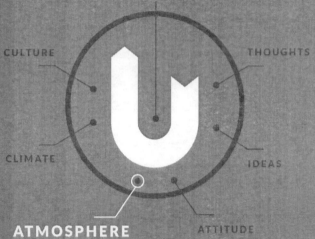

THE PROCESS OF CHANGE

CULTURE

THOUGHTS

CLIMATE

IDEAS

ATMOSPHERE

ATTITUDE

ATMOSPHERE

The swimming pool in our backyard has provided our family with countless hours of quality time, free from electronic distractions that tend to consume us when we're dry. The key is to keep the water clear, blue, and appealing all year round to attract the members of our family into the water where gadgets dare not go.

A life lesson was in order for me one morning as I walked outside, cup of coffee in hand. The fierce enemy of algae had quietly started taking its place in our family haven. Immediately, I grabbed the pole with a brush-extension in one hand while skillfully balancing my coffee in the other, launching my first attack against this enemy of our sacred family place.

After putting my back into it and providing a thorough scrub, I felt satisfied as I appreciated the blue appearance more than I had the day before. The battle continued, however, as the algae would come back in just a matter of days, and then again and again. It wasn't until I got the atmosphere of the water right by adding chemicals that the algae would stop growing. When it comes to pools, if the atmosphere is wrong, the algae grow. If the atmosphere is right, the algae stop growing.

We live in a fallen world. This fallen world naturally produces a fallen atmosphere, which naturally grows things that God never wanted in our lives. Our fleshly desires are natural inclinations that will take over the pool if we don't treat the atmosphere of our lives. Remember, the key isn't scrubbing the algae as much as it is treating the atmosphere.

Thoughts, ideas and attitudes produce the atmosphere of our lives.

To produce what God designed you to produce, you must process what God designed you to process. When you are processing God's Word and God's presence consistently, you begin to produce an atmosphere of God's kingdom in the earth. Leonard Ravenhill said, "A sinning man will stop praying, and a praying man will stop sinning."[1] The atmosphere of prayer and communication with God will not allow sin to grow. The atmosphere of sin will not allow prayer and communication with God to grow.

> Do not be misled: "Bad company corrupts good character."
>
> 1 Corinthians 15:33 (NIV)

Context is important. The atmosphere of our lives is greatly influenced by the relationships we embrace. Good character as a result of having your internal atmosphere right can still be corrupted by the wrong context of relational influence. Jesus identified with everybody, but his most intimate time was spent with lovers of God. In the context of disciples, inappropriate ideas are strangled before they become the attitude and atmosphere of the group.

Don't be misled: relationships influence what grows in the atmosphere of your life. Doug is a very close friend of mine. Many years ago, he suffered a broken neck, and as a result, he has limited mobility, living life as a quadriplegic. For two years, I assisted him in his morning routine of getting ready for his day.

One day, he suggested that I join him in his therapy wheelchair for a day at the mall to experience his challenges firsthand. Off we went to find our wives who had gone shopping hours earlier. Getting in and out of the van had its challenges, but it was nothing compared to the uphill climb from the van to the store at this particular mall. Once inside, we navigated around the mall together. Much of the time, I was holding on to the back of his electric chair, being pulled along like the caboose of a train. We were quite the pair traveling through the mall, rightfully earning the attention of many who stopped and stared.

My biggest challenge yet was our departure, when I started down the hill I had so valiantly climbed before. In what seemed like an instant, my wheelchair was speeding out of control down the inclined parking lot. Fearing for my life, I used the "Fred Flintstone technique" I'd seen as a boy growing up. I planted my feet firmly on the asphalt pavement, grinding the heels of my shoes until I came to a complete stop. As I hopped up and began pushing my wheelchair back up the hill to the van, I realized there were several people in the parking lot who were astonished at the obvious miracle they had just seen take place. This man in a wheelchair was healed before their eyes.

Doug and I have laughed many times about this experience. The reality is that our friendships affect our willingness to experiment because of the influence that grows in the atmosphere of combined thoughts, ideas, and attitudes.

Salvation occurs in a moment, but discipleship takes a lifetime. Renewing the mind is a progression and a process. There are two Greek words translating to "mind" in the following text that speak of this progression.

> Those who live according to the sinful nature have their minds set on what that nature desires; but those who live in accordance with the Spirit have their minds set on what the Spirit desires. The mind of sinful man is death, but the mind controlled by the Spirit is life and peace.
>
> Romans 8:5–6 (NIV)

Verse 5 of this passage uses the Greek word "phroneo"—this is in reference to the mind that is thinking about something. Verse 6, however, uses the Greek word "phronema," which speaks of a mind that is set or the mind that is now made up. Exercising the mind's ability to think about something results in a mindset conclusion. Marketers are constantly putting this into practice by attempting to capture our attention, which, if successful, will affect the atmosphere of our desires.

Changing your mind is not that complicated. My wife and I have many times experienced a mind set on one restaurant until we begin discussing new information about another restaurant. Many 180-Degree Turnarounds have taken place on the drive to one restaurant after new information has been introduced to the previous mindset. The process of renewing the mind occurs by consistently introducing the right information to the wrong mindset over and over until the new mindset is established. This is the process of change.

Change is a process, not an event.

To effectively experience the process of change, we must learn to serve notice on the origin of our issues rather than merely addressing the symptoms. The actions and behaviors we see have been growing in the atmosphere of our lives for years. Bringing focus and attention to a place deep beneath the obvious is essential to the process of change.

A kettle on a stove produces steam and begins to whistle, getting everybody's attention in the room. The obvious steam and whistle is what gets the attention. Dr. Jim Talley explains the fire as thoughts, the water as emotions, and the steam as behavior. Most efforts to change resemble sticking a cork in the kettle, attempting behavior modification. To truly change the atmosphere of a person's life, the thoughts and emotions that produced the behavior must be addressed.

Stop treating the symptoms, and start cultivating the atmosphere that will produce the change! When the atmosphere of your life is right, healthy living begins to result. Atmosphere sustained over the years produces a *climate*, which begins to effectively impact the lives of others.

~

Kenneth was a forty-eight-year-old single dad. He had just gotten off work and stopped to get gas on the way to pick up his son. A young man came out of the store and asked for a ride. Kenneth responded favorably to his request, and the two men left in his car. Things happened quickly. The man robbed and shot him. Kenneth was paralyzed from the waist down and is now confined to a wheelchair.

Through the process of coming to Christ, Kenneth made the choice to forgive and live again. Today, he consistently shows up to church at Destiny, offering a smile and encouragement to anybody he sees. He receives invitations to share his life message of hope and encouragement to those in The Oklahoma County Juvenile Detention Center, to injured veterans at the Oklahoma Veteran's Administration Medical Center, and in many churches.

Through a painful journey of forgiveness, the 180-Degree Turnaround of Kenneth's life resulted from his willingness to cultivate a *climate* that was pleasing to God.

Making Your 180-Degree Turnaround:

What circumstances tend to produce the wrong atmosphere for your life?

What circumstances tend to produce the right atmosphere for your life?

How can you devote yourself more effectively to pursuing the right atmosphere consistently?

CLIMATE

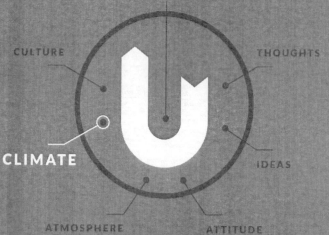

THE PROCESS OF CHANGE

CULTURE

THOUGHTS

CLIMATE

IDEAS

ATMOSPHERE

ATTITUDE

CLIMATE

Scientists can make observations and predictions of what will happen in certain climates. Several variables contribute to the climate's predictability. The consistency of a climate produces a sustainable environment for all that grows and lives there. For example, a tropical climate has the proper environment to sustain the growth of palm trees, while aspen trees grow best in the environment of high altitude and dryer air.

When Doug met Susan, their relationship began to blossom. As they fell deeper in love, they had many discussions regarding his life and needs as a quadriplegic. Finally, they both agreed that God had brought them together, and marriage was in their future. As they announced their exciting news, Doug met great resistance from Susan's Aunt Jeanie. Jeanie wanted more for her niece than this. In one conversation with Doug, Jeanie went so far as to tell him she was disappointed that Susan was marrying "less than a man." The predictability of this climate was consistently hostile, and deep hatred resulted.

They had been married for several years, and I was visiting in Doug's home. He shared with me that Aunt Jeanie still would not remain in the room when he came in. Interestingly enough, Doug's home phone began to ring.

Considering myself part of the family, I took the liberty to answer the phone. The voice was curt and very direct. It was Aunt Jeanie, and she had mistaken my voice for Doug's.

Doug and I have been friends for a very long time, and our friendship tends to find nerves and push buttons in the name of humor. As soon as I realized that I had the power to have a conversation with Aunt Jeanie in Doug's name (and with him as my audience), I took the opportunity. With the most sweet and sensitive voice I could produce, I said boldly, "Aunt Jeanie, I love you!" I received two very different responses: stunned silence on the other end of the line, and a violent reaction as Doug clicked his wheelchair into high gear, attempting to ram into my legs. I quickly concluded the phone conversation in order to defend myself against Doug's efforts to injure me physically. I had a great laugh!

A year passed by, and I was back at Doug's house when I saw something astonishing take place. Aunt Jeanie came through the door and with emotional warmth began talking, teasing, and laughing with Doug. In a few moments, it was over and she was back out the door. I was completely shocked and asked him what happened. Doug shared that my attempt to be funny a year prior had seeded something between the two of them that began to change their relationship. Slowly, the climate changed as Jeanie processed that Doug had expressed love toward her. Their relationship was transformed and they actually developed a friendship of warm appreciation.

When we nurse hurt, we grow poison.

The climate of our lives determines what grows in our future. The climate can change, but can only do so one thought at a time. Thoughts produce ideas and ideas produce attitudes. Attitudes sustained produce an atmosphere that becomes predictable about a person's life. This is the climate we grow to expect when we're around certain people.

My father grew up in a very broken home with a stepfather who, at one point, secretly offered him money to leave home. Many years of pain, anguish, and terrible mistakes would litter his life before he came to know Christ, after I had grown into an adult. I'll never forget the look on my dad's face when he shared with me what my mom's aunt told him, "Larry, there's something different about you, something very different. There's even a different look in your eye."

As he told me this, I realized it was very significant statement. There had been a lot of tension over the years with my mom's family. Aunt Betty was noticing that the predictability in my dad's life had shifted. There was a different climate in his life—a progression about who he was, what he did, how he acted, what he said, and the influence he was having in the lives of others.

Meeting Jesus is crucial to the journey of transformation in any person's life. It all begins with accepting Him as your personal savior. Accepting Jesus as your savior is a decision you make. Surrendering to Him as Lord of your life is a series of decisions you make every day for the rest of your life, as long as you live. The more surrendered you are to Christ, the more you experience a climate of God's truth restoring you to a more meaningful life.

> …you will know the truth and the truth will make you free.

> John 8:32 (NASB)

God's Word restores our minds and restores our lives one thought at a time. The more we renew our minds to His word, the less we suffer deficiency, which is the basis of dysfunction. A deficient climate produces dysfunction. A healthy climate produces restoration.

Dr. Dorothy Law Nolte referenced what grows in a child's life as a result of the climate in which they grow.

Children Learn What They Live
Dr. Dorothy Law Nolte, Ph.D. (copyright 1972)[1]

If children live with criticism, they learn to condemn.
If children live with hostility, they learn to fight.
If children live with fear, they learn to be apprehensive.
If children live with pity, they learn
to feel sorry for themselves.
If children live with ridicule, they learn to feel shy.
If children live with jealousy, they learn to feel envy.
If children live with shame, they learn to feel guilty.
If children live with encourage-
ment, they learn confidence.
If children live with tolerance, they learn patience.
If children live with praise, they learn appreciation.
If children live with acceptance, they learn to love.
If children live with approval, they
learn to like themselves.
If children live with recognition, they
learn it is good to have a goal.
If children live with sharing, they learn generosity.
If children live with honesty, they learn truthfulness.
If children live with fairness, they learn justice.
If children live with kindness and con-
sideration, they learn respect.
If children live with security, they learn to have
faith in themselves and in those about them.
If children live with friendliness, they learn
the world is a nice place in which to live.

Freedom comes when we are willing to come to a place of choosing the climate of truth more than submitting to the climate of our pain. It's easy to allow the pain of our past to hold our lives hostage.

One evening while speaking at our church, I shared a painful memory of mine as an illustration. Mrs. Robertson, my sixth grade teacher, was very aggressive in her approach to the students. It was common for her to pull my hair and thump me in the head to make a point, and admittedly, I was a problem to her in the classroom. I explained how one day Mrs. Robertson decided that public humiliation would be the best way to address my lack of interest in passing a test.

After she passed out everybody else's test, she stood at the front of the room and asked me to come before the class to get my test. She realized that I had obviously given no effort in studying for the test. As I walked in front of all my eleven-year-old peers, she purposely dropped the paper to the floor just before I grabbed it. She stood and waited until I bent down to pick up the paper and walked back to my seat. As I shared the story, to illustrate my point, I held a sheet of paper out over the platform and dropped it to the floor below.

De De Glaze, a retired teacher, sat there in the congregation that evening listening to my message, and taking note of the fallen paper. At the conclusion of the evening, I walked down from the platform and gathered my things.

Amidst all the conversations and connections that erupt following our services, Mrs. Glaze was standing there in front of me. She wasn't standing as De De, but she was there as the teacher, Mrs. Glaze. She stooped down to pick up the paper, and with a look of healing and restoration, she handed it to me. Instantly, I knew this was a spiritual transaction taking place. We embraced, and I wept in her arms that night, not even realizing the depth of emotion that still existed in my life decades after that experience.

> Let all bitterness and wrath and anger and clamor and slander be put away from you, with all malice, and be kind to one another, tenderhearted, forgiving one another, as God in Christ forgave you.
>
> Ephesians 4:31–32 (NASB)

You can choose not to let hurt become hate.

Pain wants to cripple your life, hold your mind hostage, and restrict you in subtle ways. Let it go and live again! There is an exchange taking place in our lives as we cultivate a predictable climate that allows things to grow. Nobody would ever sell their dreams for any amount, but we will exchange them if we're not careful. God never wastes a single hurt. The deeper the pain, the greater the purpose when surrendered into his loving hands. The climate of hope and anticipation of a better future will replace the climate of hurt and regret if we focus on God's purposes more than our pain.

> O magnify the LORD with me, and let us exalt His name together.
>
> Psalms 34:3 (NASB)

What you magnify in life gets bigger. Stop rehearsing your mountains to your God and start rehearsing your God to your mountains! In our fallen world, we can embrace the risen King who restores our lives and establishes a renewed *culture* in our minds and lives.

~

Nobody in my family had graduated from high school. My father was a wild character who regularly hosted drunken parties in our home. He held one hundred different jobs over the first twenty years of my life. As a child, I was sexually abused, and deficiencies were deepening in my heart and mind. Dysfunction was being translated into my life to effectively be translated to the next generation. My life changed when I met Christ, and the process of restoration began. My mom's faith was strengthened as she watched all of us come to know Christ.

Today, my entire family is serving God. I married Tracy who would graduate with honors from law school. We have two beautiful daughters and lead a wonderful ministry filled with amazing stories of God's grace. God is able to do exceedingly abundantly above and beyond all you can ask or imagine.

Making Your 180-Degree Turnaround:

What damaging climate have you been justifying in your life perhaps because you were wronged?

How willing are you to surrender that completely to God?

Who can you share this area of your life with asking them to pray in agreement with you for healing to occur?

CULTURE

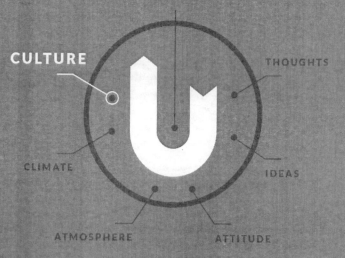

THE PROCESS OF CHANGE

CULTURE

THOUGHTS

CLIMATE

IDEAS

ATMOSPHERE

ATTITUDE

CULTURE

Like a punch in the stomach, the words rang out, "People don't change!" Respected voices in my life were unknowingly chiseling at the very foundation of who I was. The discussion grew intense as I explained that this statement was a personal assault to my changed life in Christ. People can change. People do change. Change is very misunderstood when people search for sudden results from a gradual process.

When you meet Jesus, and begin living life in the context of his strengthening, church people who know you can't believe who you were. People who knew you can't believe who you are. Change in a person's life can happen in an instant as a decision is made. Change in the culture of that person's life takes time, commitment, and community. Over time, the process of change gradually takes place.

When gradually finally arrives suddenly steals the credit.

There were so many variables that went into the transformation of my life. These are the same variables that continue to produce next-level transformation, sustaining a culture in my life that points more to Jesus every day.

What were some of the vital components of my life transformation? A relationship of ongoing communication with Christ, friendships that were loving and painfully honest at times, and a desire to recover from continued mistakes in order to move from merely existing to truly living.

It's easier to make excuses than it is to make a difference in every area of life. Somewhere, I had to stop making excuses for my behavior and start surrendering to Christ the thoughts and ideas that were producing that behavior. Circumstances are often out of your control, but your attitude is 100 percent your responsibility.

Everything you need for new life is within your reach. Jesus came teaching the kingdom of God is at hand! What's in your hand is the key to embracing all Jesus has placed within your reach. It's time to get started. God gives us his promises *as a possession.*

> And I will bring you to the land I swore with uplifted hand to give to Abraham, to Isaac and to Jacob. I will give it to you **as a possession**. I am the LORD.
>
> Exodus 6:8 (NIV)

All that you have stood for, all that you have processed in your brain over the course of your life produces the culture of who you are. This culture influences your generation and will continue to influence many generations to come.

Your decisions determine your destiny.

Your destiny is not merely the sum of your life. Your destiny involves the influence of your life into the lives of others, both now and to future generations.

Jonathan Edwards was born on October 5, 1703. He married Sarah Pierrepont, and according to *A Study in Education and Heredity* by A. E. Winship (1900),[1] their descendants included a US vice president, three US senators, three governors, three mayors, 13 college presidents, 30 judges, 65 professors, 80 public office holders, 100 lawyers, and 100 missionaries.

This same study examined the legacy of Max Jukes. He was born around 1720 and was known as a hard drinker, idle, irreverent, and uneducated. His descendants included 310 paupers, 50 women of debauchery, 400 physically wrecked by indulgent living, 7 murderers, 60 thieves, and 130 other convicts.

LEGACY

JONATHAN EDWARDS

MAX JUKES

LEGACY

LEGACY

30 JUDGES
60 AUTHORS
60 DOCTORS
100 PASTORS
100 LAWYERS
3 U.S. SENATORS
A VICE PRESIDENT
80 PUBLIC SERVANTS
75 MILITARY OFFICERS
13 COLLEGE PRESIDENTS
65 COLLEGE PROFESSORS

"You can't leave a legacy until you first live a legacy."

7 MURDERERS
150 CRIMINALS
190 PROSTITUTES
100+ ALCOHOLICS
310 DIED AS PAUPERS

There is a legacy that will be produced from the culture of your life. You can never leave a meaningful legacy until you first live a meaningful legacy. The power of our thought life has generational influence, and it's a mistake to believe that our decisions only influence our own personal destiny.

There are people who are awaiting your liberation so that they can be liberated. God has given me a new life, and in the cultural wake of this new life, I have had the privilege of proclaiming this same hope to many others. It's not something I even asked for, but somehow, in God's plan, he purposed that I would stand before crowds of people declaring His love on four continents and in several nations. This was not something I could begin to fathom earlier in the drug-riddled years of my life. We all have eternal purposes to fulfill, and when we begin to fulfill our purpose, others will discover theirs.

Generations of runners had been told that it was humanly impossible and physically dangerous to run a mile in under four minutes. In 1954, Roger Bannister was the first person to ever break this barrier, running a mile in 3 minutes, 59.4 seconds. Suddenly, the psychological barrier was broken. Within one year, sixteen more runners had done what many generations of runners could never accomplish.[2] When you begin breaking into new places of advancement, others will do the same.

> How long are you going to sit around on your hands,
> putting off taking possession of the land that God
> has given you?
>
> Joshua 18:3 (The Message)

People are waiting for you to come into the greater purposes of God for your life, and they don't even know it. God's kingdom is expanding! As we move into greater dimensions of faith and advancement, there is a breaking out to the left and to the right. On our eternal journey, God has called us to leave a trail of transformed lives!

Achieving God's promises is a cooperative effort between you and God. There is a process of developing our King's culture in our own lives. It's this culture of the King that inspires hope in all of our lives. We take the King's thoughts and ideas and adopt them as our own, actively embracing the mind of Christ (1 Cor 2:16).

> Since we have these promises, dear friends, let us
> purify ourselves from everything that contaminates
> body and spirit, perfecting holiness out of reverence
> for God.
>
> 2 Corinthians 7:1 (NIV)

As we take every thought captive and allow our ideas to be shaped by God's ideas, a certain attitude begins to result. This is the attitude of the King in you, and it stretches you into new dimensions of life.

Your attitude should be the same as that of Christ Jesus.

Philippians 2:5 (NIV)

The attitude of Christ makes way for the atmosphere of God's presence. God's presence ignites something in all of us by design. We were designed to dwell in the cultural expression of God's loving presence and participate in his divine nature. This is where the culture of dysfunction begins to be replaced with the King's culture in our lives.

His divine power has given us everything we need for life and godliness through our knowledge of him who called us by his own glory and goodness. Through these he has given us his very great and precious promises, so that through them you may participate in the divine nature and escape the corruption in the world caused by evil desires.

2 Peter 1:3–4 (NIV)

We live in a fallen world, but we serve a risen King! There is hope. You can experience a 180-Degree Turnaround, and move forward from merely existing to truly living!

Making Your 180-Degree Turnaround:

What area in your life can you identify as an area you have started losing hope for change?

What is one commitment you can make right now to take some kind of step in the direction of recovering that hope?

Who is one person you can pause to pray for right now asking God to restore them in every area of their life?

HOPE IS NOT A STRATEGY

We all hope for a brighter future and a better tomorrow, but *a dream without a strategy is just a fantasy.* To move from understanding to application requires more than hope. There must be action!

Let's be honest. The church tends to overpreach and underreach. We are all more educated than we are obedient. If all we're doing is listening to sermons, we're only getting more religious! But if we can personally translate these messages into even a fraction of action, we can change the world.

Strategic Action #1:
God's Presence Transforms Us

And we, who with unveiled faces all reflect the Lord's glory, are being transformed into his likeness with ever-increasing glory, which comes from the Lord, who is the Spirit.

2 Corinthians 3:18 (NIV)

Let your first step be to cultivate meaningful conversations of prayer every morning with God. Practice his presence as soon as you awaken. Cultivate a greater awareness of his presence all day long. Clearly, the presence of God is one of the ways our thoughts are influenced. Thoughts are the beginning of changed lives through ideas, attitudes, atmosphere, climate, and ultimately, a cultural transformation.

Surrendering daily to God's transforming presence is a constant decision of awareness. The presence of God will change the way you think and live. Formerly, I was the principal of Destiny Christian School. It was amazing how the mood of a table in the lunchroom would change as I would join the conversation. It wasn't even that the students were doing anything wrong. The mere presence of authority changes the way we behave. God's presence is with us and produces a healthy atmosphere for life.

> ...great triumph is not in your authority over evil, but in God's authority over you and presence with you. Not what you do for God but what God does for you—that's the agenda for rejoicing.
>
> Luke 10:20 (The Message)

Consider the last time you were driving, and you saw a police car. Suddenly, and almost without thinking, your foot comes off the accelerator and is prepared to hit the brakes. The presence of authority affects our behavior. The reality is that the police car was there before you realized it was there. When you became aware of the police car is when you were influenced. It's not the presence of God but rather the awareness of the presence of God that will change our lives.

For the time will come when all the earth will be filled, as the waters fill the sea, with an awareness of the glory of the LORD.

Habakkuk 2:14 (NLT)

Strategic Action #2: God's Word Transforms Us

And do not be conformed to this world, but be transformed by the renewing of your mind, so that you may prove what the will of God is, that which is good and acceptable and perfect.

Romans 12:2 (NASB)

Consistently rehearse the truths of God's Word. As God's thoughts become your thoughts, God's ideas will become your ideas. God's attitude looks into darkness and calls for light! This becomes your attitude, and the atmosphere of faith begins to be the expression of your life. The climate of his transforming power expresses the culture of God's kingdom in you and through you.

God's promises unlock God's potential in God's people! It's God's plan for us to actually participate in the divine nature of God through the promises of his Word.

His divine power has given us everything we need for life and godliness through our knowledge of him who called us by his own glory and goodness.

Through these he has given us his very great and precious promises, so that through them you may participate in the divine nature and escape the corruption in the world caused by evil desires.

2 Peter 1:3–4 (NIV)

We have been empowered by God to take up his promises as weapons against a fallen world's perspective. Rehearsing, memorizing, and actively meditating on God's Word produces the victorious perspective of a risen king even in our fallen world.

Since we have these promises, dear friends, let us purify ourselves from everything that contaminates body and spirit, perfecting holiness out of reverence for God.

2 Corinthians 7:1 (NIV)

Practical reminders have helped me over the years to more actively engage in God's Word. Index cards with key verses that I've carried in my pocket reminded me of God's Word every time I reach for money to make a purchase. Verses I lay on my bed to rehearse before going to sleep at night. Sticky notes on my mirror have reminded me over the years to wake myself up spiritually when waking up physically. Calendar email reminders, pop-up reminders, passwords pointing to a promise, and many other practical things to keep my brain on track all day long.

Every day, as I read my Bible, I write the date at the top of the page where I stopped reading before, and I add anything special about that day like, "Faith took her first steps last night." Just reading two pages a day is an easy enough goal that I can accomplish almost every day of the year. When I can read more, I do but doing this daily has helped me stay the course and has now, years later, given me Bibles with all kinds of treasured memories written on the pages. Hopefully, one day, my grandchildren will be impacted by my love for God's Word as they look through these heirlooms—pages of Scripture that have not only comingled with my life, but have become the expression of my life.

Strategic Action #3:
God's People Transform Us

May your next step be to cultivate meaningful relationships.

> ...our marvelous God whose gracious Word can make you into what he wants you to be and give you everything you could possibly need in this community of holy friends.
>
> Acts 20:32 (The Message)

For years, Monterey, California, was a pelican's paradise. As the fishermen cleaned their fish, the birds feasted on all that was left over. The birds became fat and lazy having grown dependent upon the fishermen's continued practices.

Eventually, these scraps were utilized, and the practice of feeding the pelicans ceased. No longer in the practice of fishing for themselves, many pelicans starved to death. New pelicans were imported from the south and placed among their starving relatives. These new arrivals immediately started catching fish. The process of mentoring had begun, and before long, the famine was ended.[1]

Build a circle to break a cycle. God's plan for our lives is a community plan. Jesus came into the earth declaring that God is our Father, and God's children are our brothers and sisters. He brought the greatest revelation of family and community the world had ever known. When he taught the disciples to pray, he told them to use words like "Our Father," "Give us this day," "Our daily bread," "Forgive us," "our debts," and "as we forgive."

There are dangerous attitudes of disconnection from the church in our world today. It has become somewhat fashionable to be independent and hold critical views of the church. As long as pastors are blaming people and people are blaming pastors, hostility hinders health and progress.

Studies performed by Ronald Glaser, of the Ohio State University College of Medicine, and psychologist Janice Kiecolt-Glaser investigated the effect that stress associated with marital strife has on the healing of wounds, a significant marker of genetic activation. The researchers created small suction blisters on the skin of married test subjects, after which each couple was instructed to have a neutral discussion for half an hour. For the next three weeks, the researchers then monitored the production of three of the proteins that our bodies produce in association with wound healing.[2]

We are designed for healthy, loving, nurturing, gracious, and forgiving relationships. It's human to make a mistake. It's divine to overlook the offense and to stay the course with the connection. From the very beginning, God revealed that it is not good for man to be alone! We are called to each other and are part of each other's destiny.

> For just as we have many members in one body and all the members do not have the same function, so we, who are many, are one body in Christ, and individually members one of another.
>
> Romans 12:4–5 (NASB)

> In this way we are like the various parts of a human body. Each part gets its meaning from the body as a whole, not the other way around.
>
> Romans 12:4 (The Message)

Christianity and the church are inseparable. You are lacking purpose and violating your design if you are not a contributing part of a local church family. We are all part of the universal church. We are also part of universal humanity, but we have a local family into which we were born which is imperfect.

A family is functional and healthy when each member of the family becomes a servant. A family is dysfunctional and unhealthy when members of the family become selfish. Together, we make our family a wonderful place as we serve by putting away dishes, preparing for guests, and helping each other along the journey. If church has never felt like family to you, perhaps it's because you've never really served there.

> He is in charge of it all, has the final word on eve-erything. At the center of all this, Christ rules the church. The church, you see, is not peripheral to the world; the world is peripheral to the church. The church is Christ's body, in which he speaks and acts, by which he fills everything with his presence.
>
> Ephesians 1:22–23 (The Message)

My prayer for you is that you move from merely existing to truly living. May God's presence, God's Word, and God's people transform the culture of your life one thought at a time.

180° TURNAROUND

THE PROCESS OF CHANGE

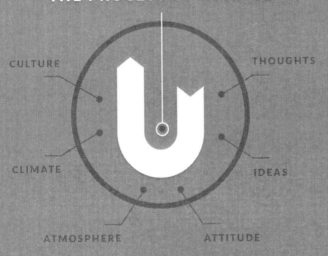

CULTURE

THOUGHTS

CLIMATE

IDEAS

ATMOSPHERE

ATTITUDE

Thoughts sustained produce ideas. Ideas sustained produce attitudes. Attitudes sustained produce an atmosphere. Atmosphere sustained produces a climate. Climate sustained produces culture. Culture resulting from the thoughts and wisdom of God is the expression of God's Kingdom in the earth through our surrendered lives!

MORE 180-DEGREE TURNAROUND STORIES

Debra was in and out of five county jails, rehabs, and prison for drug charges. She lost her home, children, and her entire family. She came to know the hope of Christ while serving time. After her last sentence, Debra discovered a church family that would surround her by providing home repairs, food, tutoring, and whatever was needed. When she first came to Destiny, she could barely communicate verbally, let alone intelligibly. Debra has since graduated with a college degree, she owns her own home, and God has restored her mind and emotions. She is actively involved as a contributing member of the Destiny family and is making a difference in other people's lives. At the time this book is being written, she's been clean for seven years! Jesus and his church changes lives! God has restored her relationship with her sons and other family members.

~

Gena's broken family life drove her to drug and alcohol abuse. At one point, she woke up after a week of heavy parties and couldn't remember how to spell her own name. This was a turning point away from drugs but the alcoholism continued. At twenty-three, Gena finally came to realize that Jesus really did exist, and he loved her uncon- ditionally. Suddenly, she became an outcast from her fam- ily as they did not understand this new life of happiness she had found. Gena and James continued to place Christ at the center of their lives and their marriage, and after twenty-five years of marriage are still very in love. They have four children who are now adults and have been raised in their Christian home with Christian values. Gena's fam- ily understands that God can truly forgive no matter what a person's past may be.

~

At age sixteen, Rebecca was raped. Feeling no self-worth, she started working in the strip clubs by the age of eight- een. Soon, she was selling her body in the clubs and later with an escort service. Drug abuse followed as an attempt to dull the pain she felt in her heart. Life was void and empty in every way. Rebecca came to Christ and began growing in her relationship with God. This began to cause that empty void to slowly disappear. Today, Rebecca and her three sons are very involved in the ministries of Destiny Christian Center and are helping to make a difference in other people's lives. Recently, Rebecca graduated from col- lege with her degree and is continuing on with her educa- tion as she seeks God for his wisdom and guidance for her life and family!

~

Ryan was twenty-two years old and had just come out of a failed marriage. Before leaving for an air force temporary duty assignment, he took a bet. While away on a ninety-day advance school, Ryan had wagered that he could sleep with ninety women. Some people struggle with drugs, alcohol, or even shopping. For Ryan, it was sex. God, however, had different plans. Soon after getting to Denver, he was arrested and then released quickly. It was then that he met Gena. To Ryan, she was just another score, but God had divinely brought Gena into his life. Gena's heart for Christ and commitment to purity had a deep and immediate impact on Ryan's life. Ryan grew up in a Lutheran church, never having accepted Christ until he met Gena. Today, Ryan and Gena are part of the leadership team at Destiny and are dramatically impacting lives of people from every walk and background.

~

Janie was raised in the foster care system after suffering severe physical and sexual abuse as a child. She was left feeling unwanted and not good enough. Her low self esteem and painful past led her to alcohol and drugs. Her brother was murdered by his father, and another brother died in a biking accident. Her conclusion was that nobody cared and that God hated her. Layers of hate formed over layers of pain, and Janie felt unlovable, worthless, and abandoned. After becoming pregnant with her first child, she decided to try going to church on his behalf. In this atmosphere of God's family, Janie's heart began to change. She gave her life to Christ, and the process of healing began. God restored relationships that seemed completely lost and continues to heal hurts using the pain of her past to help others have courage in their lives. Janie is faithful to show up early at Destiny always offering a smile and laughter to everybody she touches.

~

Having grown up in an angry and abusive home, Dennis found himself addicted to all kinds of drugs, homeless, and living in an abandoned garage. Being a U.S. Navy veteran and possessing a college degree, he had only existed on odd jobs here and there to get his next high for a long time. Eventually, he turned to crime to support his lifestyle. After several arrests he was waiting to go to prison when he met a lady who introduced him to Jesus through her song. He began attending Church on occasion and something miraculous began to happen inside him. His recovery from a lifetime of drug addiction has been progressive but God has used his progression as a living example of how relying on Jesus can truly change somebody from the inside out. Dennis found Destiny Christian Center, a church family who embraced him just as he was. Today he is married to an amazing woman, has 4 children and a great job as the chief financial officer of a large delivery service.

~

Darla was fifteen, pregnant, and just married to Larry, who had grown up in an abusive environment. He was very insecure, had no self-esteem, and would become an abusive husband and father himself. They had a daughter and a son within three years and Darla would always take them to church. As they got older, the kids ran from God. Darla's son got involved with drugs while her daughter had emotional issues and continued to try and fill that void with multiple marriages. After being married for twenty years, they actually decided to have another child, and Chris was born. He was destined to have a different dad and family atmosphere than the older two had grown up knowing. Their older son, Lawrence gave his heart to Jesus first. Then he and Darla fasted and prayed together consistently for Larry, and that same year, he surrendered his life to Christ. The three of them prayed together for their oldest child, Laura, and several years later, she was radically saved. Today, almost fifty years into the marriage, Larry and Darla are serving the Lord together in the church where Lawrence, their oldest son, is the lead pastor, and Chris, their youngest son, is the youth pastor. Laura lives in a different city but has an amazing passion for God and is a ministry leader, directing Celebrate Recovery with her husband in their church. Though only being married once, Darla has actually had two husbands. "Therefore, if anyone is in Christ, he is a new creation, the old has gone, the new has come" (2 Cor 5:17, NIV, 1984).

~

Entire families can come to Christ and make the world a better place! God is "able to do exceedingly abundantly above all that we ask or think, according to the power that works in us." (Eph 3:20, NKJV).

We are God's family. The family of the forgiven!

ENDNOTES

Ideas

1 "Democracy." In Encyclopedia Britannica Online.
2 Aristotle, *Politics*, http://classics.mit.edu/Aristotle/politics.6.six.html (accessed), 1317b (book 6, part II).

Attitude

1 Famous Failures motivational video, copyright BluefishTV.com
2 Jim Clemmer, *Growing the Distance: Timeless Principles for Personal, Career and Family Success*, (Ontario, Canada: The Clemmer Group, 1999).
3 http://www.examiner.com/article/many-children-laugh-a-lot-every-day-even-if-no-one-is-telling-a-joke

Atmosphere

1 Ravenhill, Leonard. *Why Revival Tarries*, (Bloomington, MN: Bethany House, 2004).

Climate

1 Dorothy Nolte, *Children Learn What They Live*, (1972) http://www.empowermentresources.com/info2/children-learn-long_version.html (accessed).

Culture

[1] Winship, A. E. *A Study in Education and Heredity*. 1900.

[2] Lowitt, Bruce. "Bannister Stuns World With 4-Minute Mile." © *St. Petersburg Times*. December 17, 1999.

Hope is Not a Strategy

[1] *Bits and Pieces*. June 23, 1994. p. 17

[2] Dawson Church, *The Genie in Your Genes: Epigenetic Medicine and the New Biology of Intention*, (Fulton, CA: Energy Psychology Press, 2009).